# LOOK INSIDE
# CROSS-SECTIONS
# RECORD
## BREAKERS

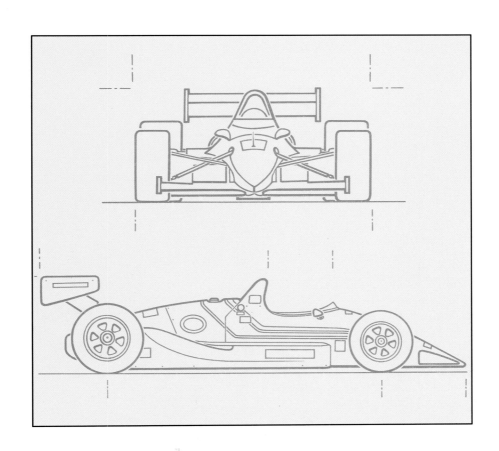

# LOOK INSIDE
# CROSS-SECTIONS
# RECORD
## BREAKERS

ILLUSTRATED BY
## CHRIS GRIGG AND KEITH HARMER

WRITTEN BY
## MOIRA BUTTERFIELD

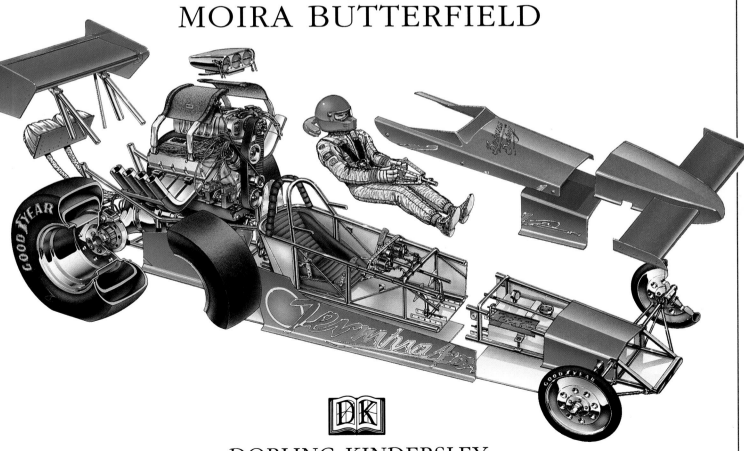

## DORLING KINDERSLEY
LONDON • NEW YORK • STUTTGART

A DORLING KINDERSLEY BOOK

**Art Editor** Dorian Spencer Davies
**Designer** Sharon Grant, Sara Hill
**Senior Art Editor** C. David Gillingwater
**Project Editor** Constance Novis
**Senior Editor** John C. Miles
**U.S. Editor** Camela Decaire
**Production** Louise Barratt

First American edition, 1995
2 4 6 8 10 9 7 5 3 1
Published in the United States
by Dorling Kindersley Publishing, Inc.,
95 Madison Avenue, New York, New York 10016

Copyright © 1995 Dorling Kindersley Limited, London

A catalog record is available from
the Library of Congress

ISBN 0-7894-0320-X.

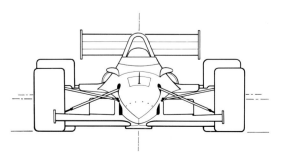

Reproduced by Dot Gradations, Essex
Printed and bound by Proost, Belgium

# CONTENTS

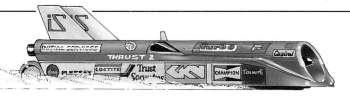

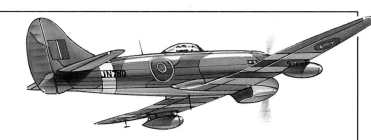

# BLACKBIRD

**ON JULY 25, 1964, PRESIDENT LYNDON JOHNSON** of the United States announced a new aircraft development program. The airplane in question would be used for spying and reconnaissance (taking photographs of enemy territory). It would be equipped with the most sophisticated electronic and surveillance systems and would fly higher and faster than any other airplane. The result of the program looked like nothing else in the air. Painted deep blue-black, the new aircraft was officially called the SR-71, but it quickly became popularly known as the "Blackbird." It still holds several air speed records today.

## Speed machine

The SR-71 was designed to fly both higher and faster than any other aircraft. Its maximum speed was Mach 3.2, or more than three times the speed of sound. This is equivalent to more than 2,100 mph (3,300 km/h).

## High heat

Much of the SR-71 was made of titanium, a metal used in spacecraft. Titanium is immensely strong and very resistant to the heat generated at high speeds.

Forward titanium cockpit canopy

Rear cockpit canopy

Radar absorbing wedge

Fuselage fuel tank

Ejector seat

Midair refueling receptacle

Systems operator

Pilot

Rear cockpit

Forward cockpit

Pitot tube

Technical objective camera

Electronics package

Engine inlet spike

Forward landing gear

Leading edge wing structure

Side-looking radar compartment

Liquid oxygen tank

Rear cockpit electronics

Platform computer

Environmental control system

## Blackbirds

The SR-71 was painted blue-black to radiate the intense heat generated by friction from air rubbing against the aircraft at high speed. The paint used on the SR-71 also had minute iron balls in it that helped confuse enemy radar.

## Flying suits

The two-man crew of the SR-71 wore special flying suits. The suits protected them from the stresses of flying at high altitudes where the Earth's atmosphere is very thin. They also ate low-gas foods to prevent them from developing crippling abdominal cramps due to air pressure differences. Because the flying suits were difficult to put on, the crew members "suited up" in a support van and were driven to the aircraft.

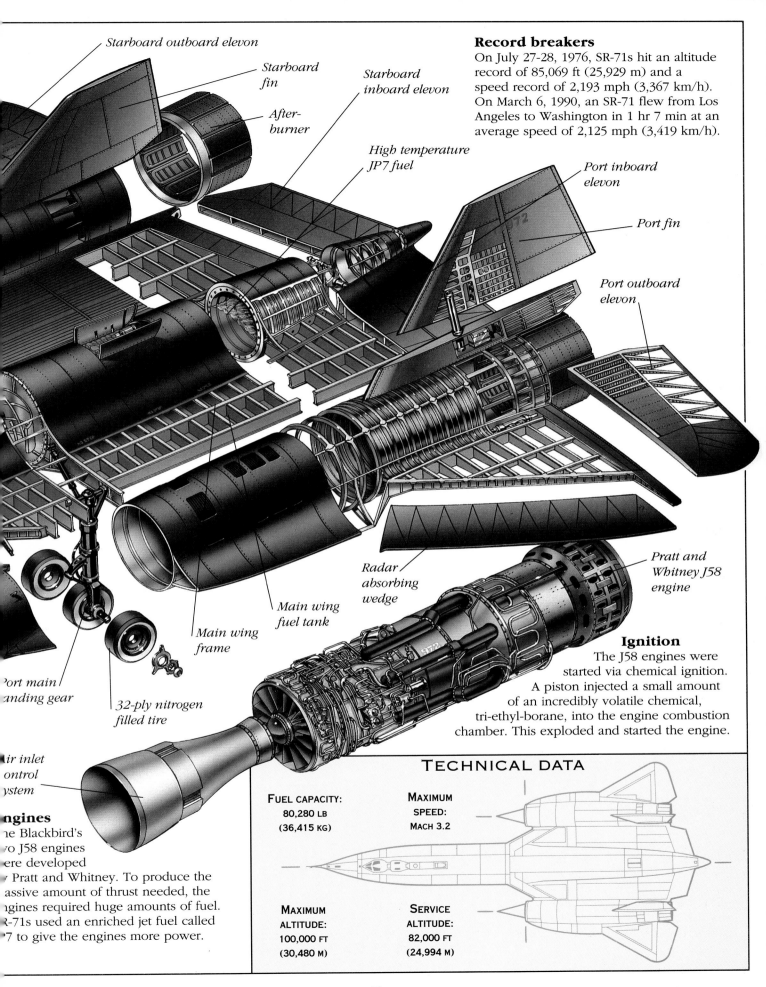

Starboard outboard elevon

Starboard fin

After-burner

Starboard inboard elevon

High temperature JP7 fuel

**Record breakers**
On July 27-28, 1976, SR-71s hit an altitude record of 85,069 ft (25,929 m) and a speed record of 2,193 mph (3,367 km/h). On March 6, 1990, an SR-71 flew from Los Angeles to Washington in 1 hr 7 min at an average speed of 2,125 mph (3,419 km/h).

Port inboard elevon

Port fin

Port outboard elevon

Radar absorbing wedge

Main wing fuel tank

Main wing frame

Port main landing gear

32-ply nitrogen filled tire

Air inlet control system

Pratt and Whitney J58 engine

**Ignition**
The J58 engines were started via chemical ignition. A piston injected a small amount of an incredibly volatile chemical, tri-ethyl-borane, into the engine combustion chamber. This exploded and started the engine.

**Engines**
The Blackbird's two J58 engines were developed by Pratt and Whitney. To produce the massive amount of thrust needed, the engines required huge amounts of fuel. SR-71s used an enriched jet fuel called JP7 to give the engines more power.

## TECHNICAL DATA

| | |
|---|---|
| **FUEL CAPACITY:** 80,280 LB (36,415 KG) | **MAXIMUM SPEED:** MACH 3.2 |
| **MAXIMUM ALTITUDE:** 100,000 FT (30,480 M) | **SERVICE ALTITUDE:** 82,000 FT (24,994 M) |

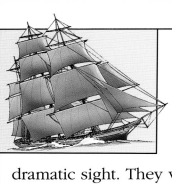

# TEA CLIPPER

THE TEA CLIPPERS WERE SOME OF THE FASTEST SAILING SHIPS ever built. Their elegant shape helped them carve a fast path through the water, and with all their sails hoisted, they made a dramatic sight. They were built to carry tea from China to England during the mid-19th century. The demand for each new season's crop of tea meant that the first ship into port could get a very high price for its cargo. Interest in races between the ships built up in the newspapers, and clippers became internationally famous.

### Short-lived stardom

The heyday of the clippers was in the 1860s, but it was short-lived. The rise of steamships and the opening of the Suez Canal in 1869 shortened the journey from China, and sailing ships could not use the canal. Clippers were forced to seek other cargoes, such as wool from Australia.

### Iron ribs

Clipper ship designers faced big problems. Wood was heavy and becoming scarce. Iron was light and strong, but poor ventilation in iron-hulled ships damaged the tea. The answer was a composite hull made of wood planking on an iron frame.

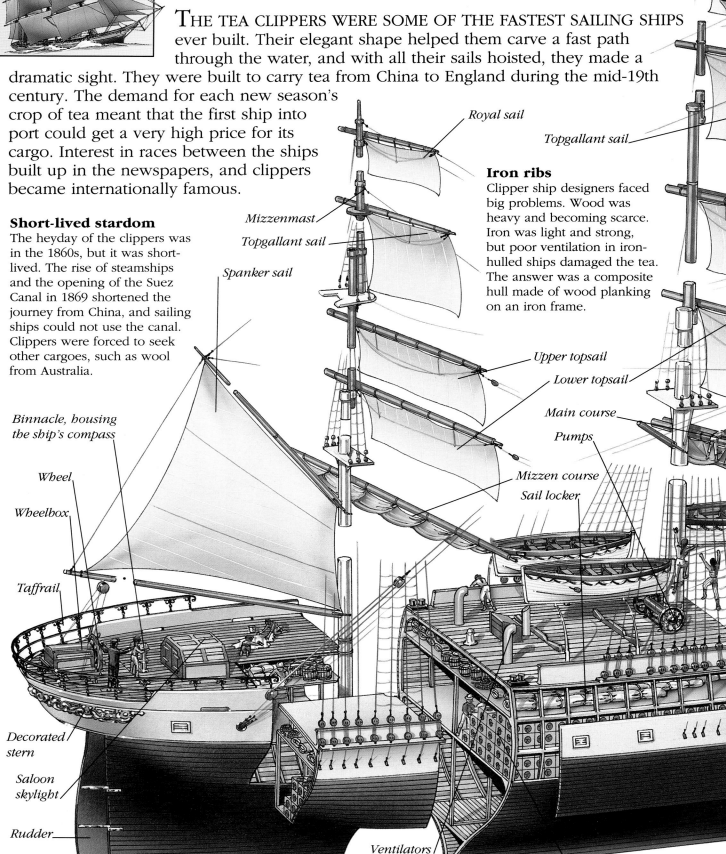

Skysail

Royal sail

Topgallant sail

Mizzenmast

Topgallant sail

Spanker sail

Upper topsail

Lower topsail

Main course

Pumps

Binnacle, housing the ship's compass

Mizzen course

Sail locker

Wheel

Wheelbox

Taffrail

Decorated stern

Saloon skylight

Rudder

Ventilators

Cargo of tea packed in ches

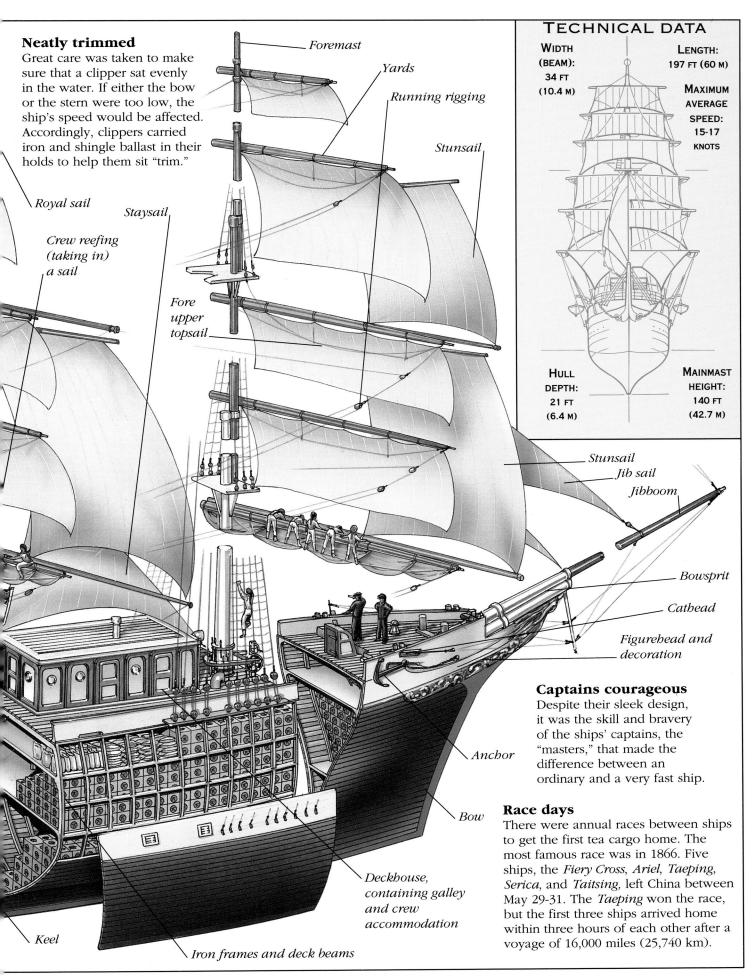

**Neatly trimmed**
Great care was taken to make sure that a clipper sat evenly in the water. If either the bow or the stern were too low, the ship's speed would be affected. Accordingly, clippers carried iron and shingle ballast in their holds to help them sit "trim."

*Foremast*

*Yards*

*Running rigging*

*Stunsail*

*Royal sail*

*Staysail*

*Crew reefing (taking in) a sail*

*Fore upper topsail*

*Stunsail*

*Jib sail*

*Jibboom*

*Bowsprit*

*Cathead*

*Figurehead and decoration*

*Anchor*

*Bow*

*Deckhouse, containing galley and crew accommodation*

*Keel*

*Iron frames and deck beams*

**Captains courageous**
Despite their sleek design, it was the skill and bravery of the ships' captains, the "masters," that made the difference between an ordinary and a very fast ship.

**Race days**
There were annual races between ships to get the first tea cargo home. The most famous race was in 1866. Five ships, the *Fiery Cross, Ariel, Taeping, Serica,* and *Taitsing,* left China between May 29-31. The *Taeping* won the race, but the first three ships arrived home within three hours of each other after a voyage of 16,000 miles (25,740 km).

# DRAGSTER

THE RACE IS ABOUT TO BEGIN AND TWO LONG, LEAN dragster cars edge forward to the starting line. The lights turn green and the cars leap away. Top Fuel dragsters such as the one show here can move fast – the record time is 4.726 seconds to cover quarter mile (402 m). At the end of this record-breaking r the car's speed was 308.64 mph (496.7 km/h)!

Rear airfoil

Airfoil side panel

Blower bag

"Bug catcher" air inlet manifold for blower

Super-charger

Supercharger drive bel

Padded headrest

Support strut

Parachutes

4,000 hp V8 engine

Quick-release shoulder harness

Rear tire made of soft rubber compound

Thin sidewalls

Inner tire for stability

Rear wheel

Header (exhaust manifold)

Disc brake

Battery

Roll cage

Cockpit

Decorated bodywork

Parachute release lever

## Blowers and fuel

Top Fuel dragsters are so named because they are fueled by a mixture of nitromethane and methanol very different from the fuel in an ordinary car. This mixture gives more power to an engine than ordinary fuel can. The cars also have supercharged engines, called blowers. A supercharger gives even more power to the engine by forcing a fuel vapor/air mixture into it under greatly increased pressure.

## Burnout!

One of the most spectacular sights in drag racing is the burnout. As part of the pre-race preparations, the rear tires are lubricated with water and made to spin very quickly. This cleans and heats them to their melting point, making them very sticky. It also lays a carpet of rubber across the starting line. All of this helps the dragster gain extra grip for the crucial fast start.

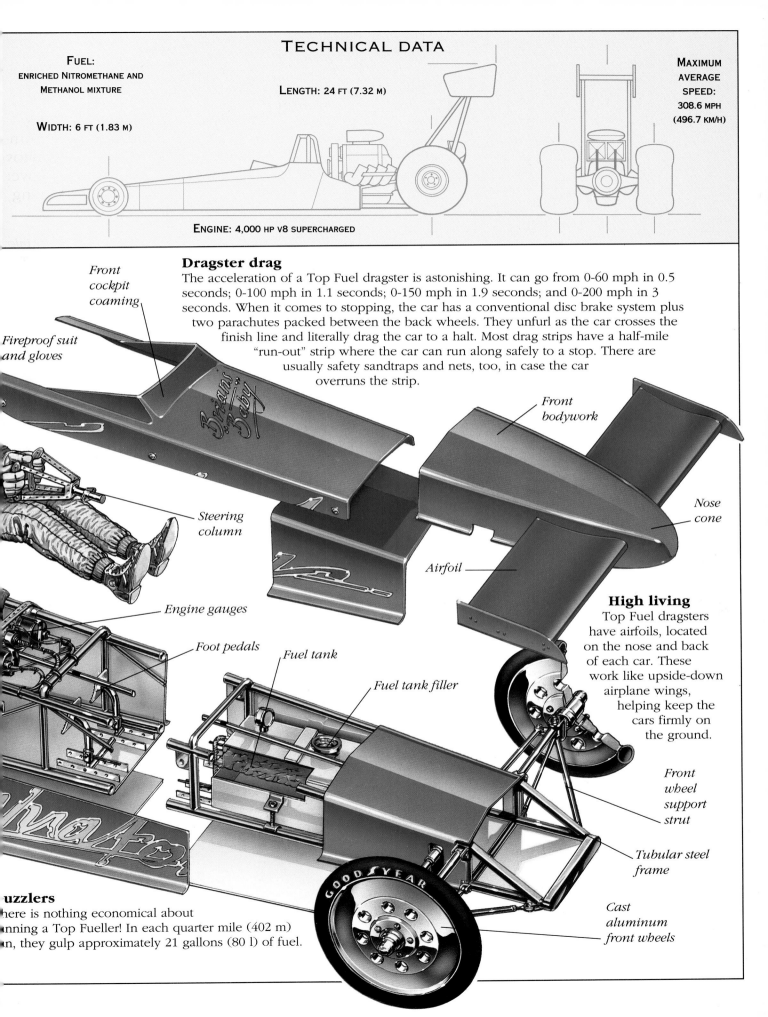

## TECHNICAL DATA

**FUEL:**
ENRICHED NITROMETHANE AND
METHANOL MIXTURE

**WIDTH: 6 FT (1.83 M)**

**LENGTH: 24 FT (7.32 M)**

**MAXIMUM AVERAGE SPEED: 308.6 MPH (496.7 KM/H)**

**ENGINE: 4,000 HP V8 SUPERCHARGED**

### Dragster drag
The acceleration of a Top Fuel dragster is astonishing. It can go from 0-60 mph in 0.5 seconds; 0-100 mph in 1.1 seconds; 0-150 mph in 1.9 seconds; and 0-200 mph in 3 seconds. When it comes to stopping, the car has a conventional disc brake system plus two parachutes packed between the back wheels. They unfurl as the car crosses the finish line and literally drag the car to a halt. Most drag strips have a half-mile "run-out" strip where the car can run along safely to a stop. There are usually safety sandtraps and nets, too, in case the car overruns the strip.

*Front cockpit coaming*

*Fireproof suit and gloves*

*Brians Baby*

*Steering column*

*Engine gauges*

*Foot pedals*

*Fuel tank*

*Fuel tank filler*

*Front bodywork*

*Nose cone*

*Airfoil*

### High living
Top Fuel dragsters have airfoils, located on the nose and back of each car. These work like upside-down airplane wings, helping keep the cars firmly on the ground.

*Front wheel support strut*

*Tubular steel frame*

*Cast aluminum front wheels*

**uzzlers**
here is nothing economical about
nning a Top Fueller! In each quarter mile (402 m)
n, they gulp approximately 21 gallons (80 l) of fuel.

# PWC

IN 1968 AN AMERICAN MOTORCYCLE racer named Clay Jacobson had a bright idea. He was fed up with the cuts and bruises he got from falling off his bike onto hard ground, so he designed a machine that combined the thrill of motorcycling with the skills of waterskiing – it guaranteed a softer landing when he fell off! The idea of the "personal watercraft," or PWC for short, was born. Jacobson developed some prototypes with the Kawasaki company, using snowmobile engines. The first Kawasaki Jet Ski came into production in 1973, and now PWCs are a common sight at beaches and lakefronts all over the world, speeding across the water and sending up plumes of spray as their riders carve quick turns.

*Handlebar*

*Throttle control*

*Engine compartment cover*

## Pump power

The PWC shown here is powered by a 530 cc engine that drives a three-bladed "impeller," an internal propeller, mounted in a pump at the back of the craft. Water coming in through an opening in the bottom of the hull is forced out through a narrow nozzle as the impeller spins around. This creates a jet of water that pushes the craft along. This model has a cruising speed of about 35 mph (56.3 km/h).

*Deck fins*

*Fire extinguisher in compartment*

*Riding tray*

*Jet nozzle pump*

*Impeller*

*Fuel switch*

*Drive shaft*

*Choke control*

*Exhaust outlet*

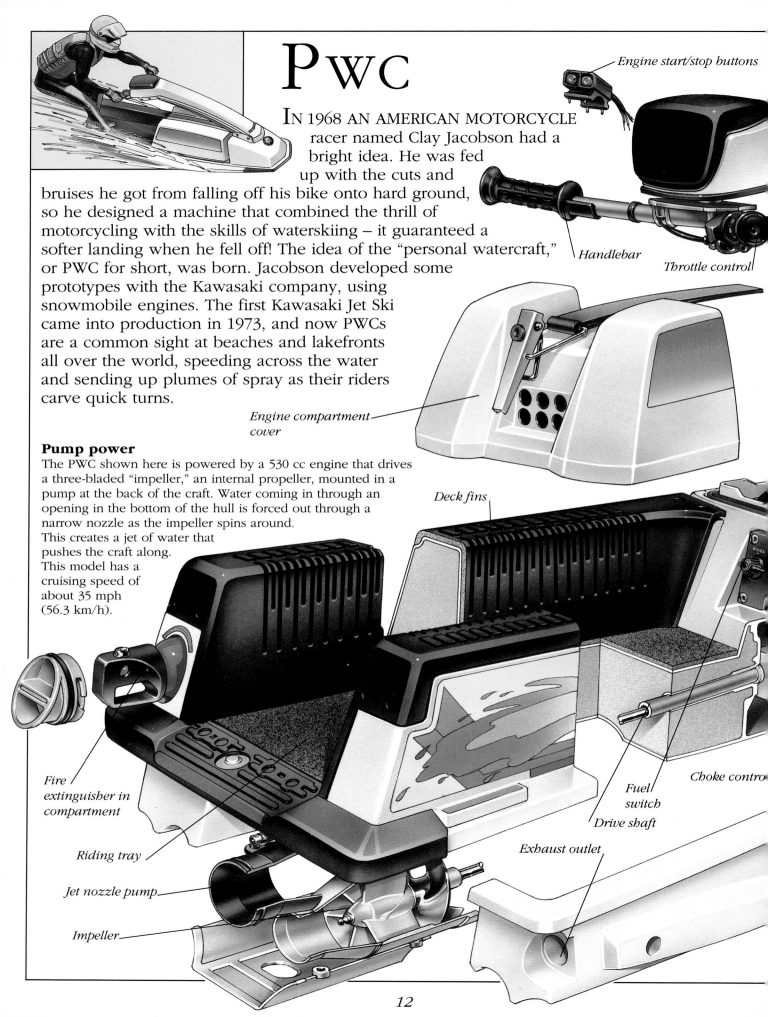

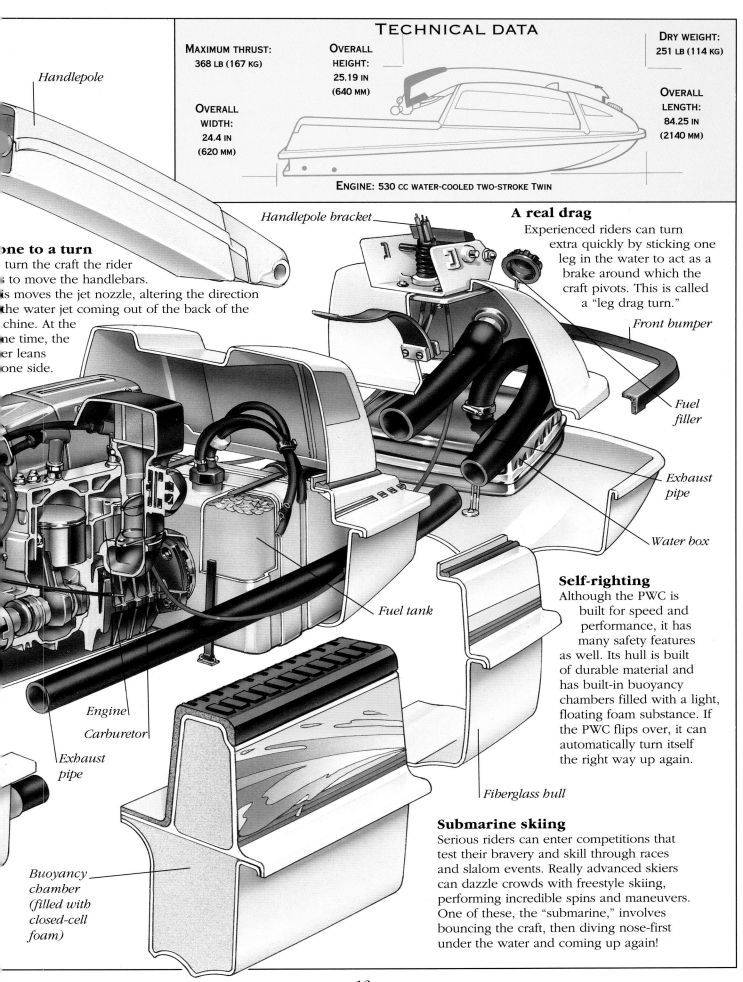

**MAXIMUM THRUST:**
368 LB (167 KG)

**OVERALL HEIGHT:**
25.19 IN (640 MM)

**DRY WEIGHT:**
251 LB (114 KG)

**OVERALL WIDTH:**
24.4 IN (620 MM)

**OVERALL LENGTH:**
84.25 IN (2140 MM)

**ENGINE: 530 CC WATER-COOLED TWO-STROKE TWIN**

*Handlepole*

*Handlepole bracket*

### one to a turn

turn the craft the rider s to move the handlebars. is moves the jet nozzle, altering the direction the water jet coming out of the back of the chine. At the ne time, the er leans one side.

### A real drag

Experienced riders can turn extra quickly by sticking one leg in the water to act as a brake around which the craft pivots. This is called a "leg drag turn."

*Front bumper*

*Fuel filler*

*Exhaust pipe*

*Water box*

*Fuel tank*

*Engine*

*Carburetor*

*Exhaust pipe*

### Self-righting

Although the PWC is built for speed and performance, it has many safety features as well. Its hull is built of durable material and has built-in buoyancy chambers filled with a light, floating foam substance. If the PWC flips over, it can automatically turn itself the right way up again.

*Fiberglass hull*

### Submarine skiing

Serious riders can enter competitions that test their bravery and skill through races and slalom events. Really advanced skiers can dazzle crowds with freestyle skiing, performing incredible spins and maneuvers. One of these, the "submarine," involves bouncing the craft, then diving nose-first under the water and coming up again!

*Buoyancy chamber (filled with closed-cell foam)*

# THRUST 2

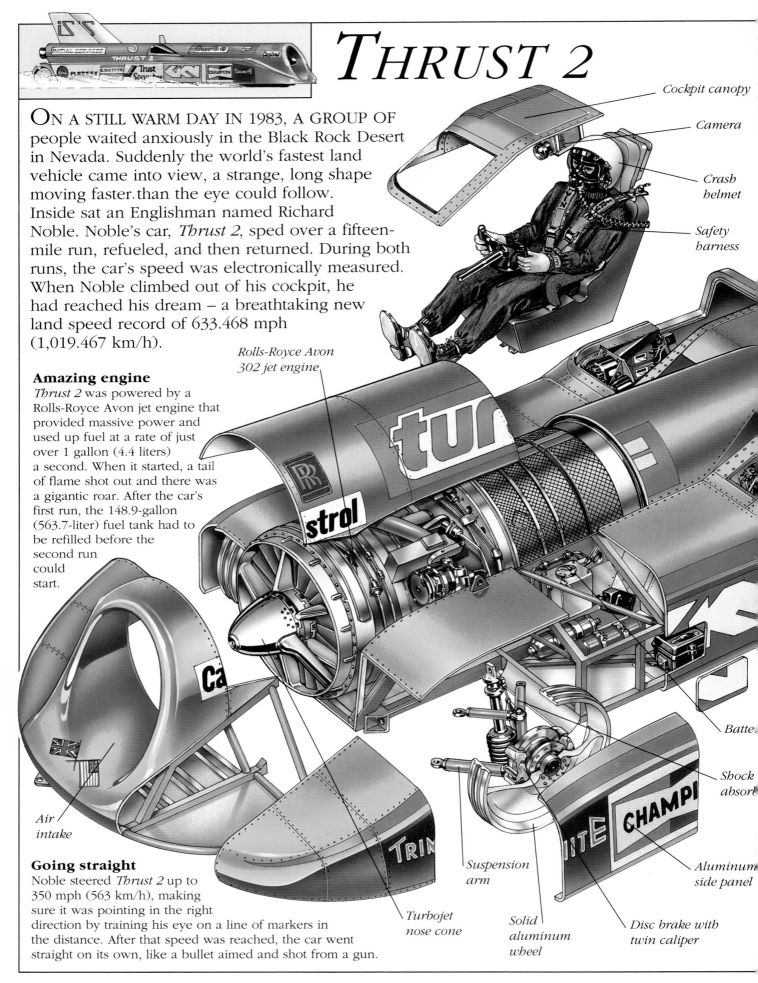

**Cockpit canopy**

**Camera**

**Crash helmet**

**Safety harness**

ON A STILL WARM DAY IN 1983, A GROUP OF people waited anxiously in the Black Rock Desert in Nevada. Suddenly the world's fastest land vehicle came into view, a strange, long shape moving faster.than the eye could follow. Inside sat an Englishman named Richard Noble. Noble's car, *Thrust 2*, sped over a fifteen-mile run, refueled, and then returned. During both runs, the car's speed was electronically measured. When Noble climbed out of his cockpit, he had reached his dream – a breathtaking new land speed record of 633.468 mph (1,019.467 km/h).

## Amazing engine

*Thrust 2* was powered by a Rolls-Royce Avon jet engine that provided massive power and used up fuel at a rate of just over 1 gallon (4.4 liters) a second. When it started, a tail of flame shot out and there was a gigantic roar. After the car's first run, the 148.9-gallon (563.7-liter) fuel tank had to be refilled before the second run could start.

**Rolls-Royce Avon 302 jet engine**

**Air intake**

## Going straight

Noble steered *Thrust 2* up to 350 mph (563 km/h), making sure it was pointing in the right direction by training his eye on a line of markers in the distance. After that speed was reached, the car went straight on its own, like a bullet aimed and shot from a gun.

**Turbojet nose cone**

**Suspension arm**

**Solid aluminum wheel**

**Disc brake with twin caliper**

**Aluminum side panel**

**Shock absorber**

**Batte**

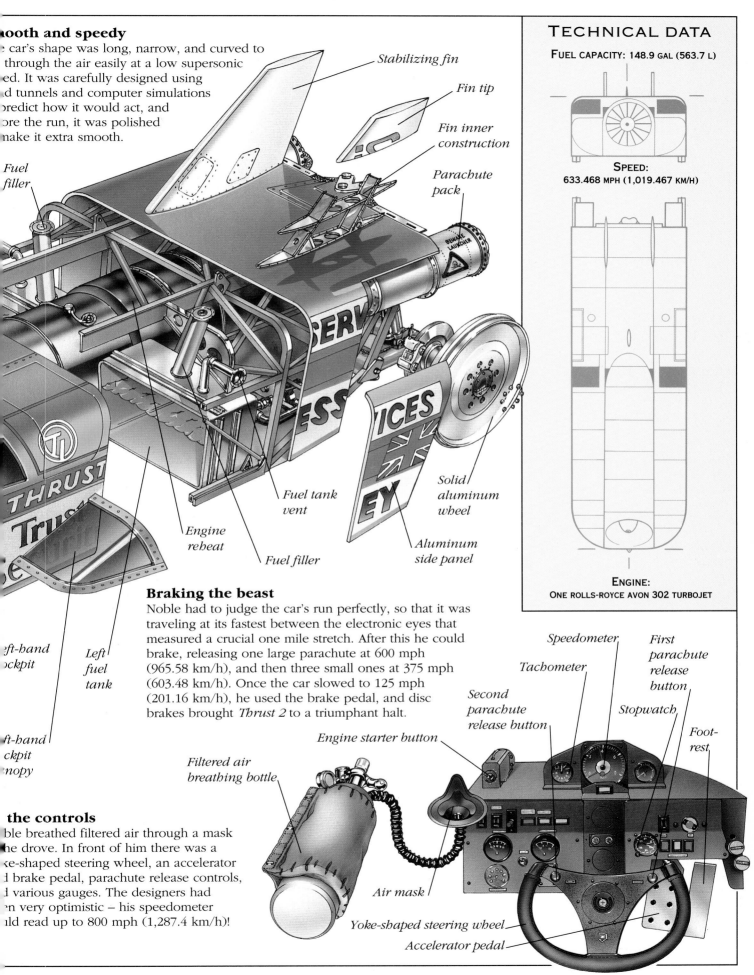

## ...ooth and speedy

...e car's shape was long, narrow, and curved to ...through the air easily at a low supersonic ...ed. It was carefully designed using ...d tunnels and computer simulations ...redict how it would act, and ...ore the run, it was polished ...make it extra smooth.

*Fuel filler*

*Stabilizing fin*

*Fin tip*

*Fin inner construction*

*Parachute pack*

*Fuel tank vent*

*Engine reheat*

*Fuel filler*

*Solid aluminum wheel*

*Aluminum side panel*

*ft-hand ckpit*

*Left fuel tank*

*ft-hand ckpit nopy*

### Braking the beast

Noble had to judge the car's run perfectly, so that it was traveling at its fastest between the electronic eyes that measured a crucial one mile stretch. After this he could brake, releasing one large parachute at 600 mph (965.58 km/h), and then three small ones at 375 mph (603.48 km/h). Once the car slowed to 125 mph (201.16 km/h), he used the brake pedal, and disc brakes brought *Thrust 2* to a triumphant halt.

*Speedometer*

*Tachometer*

*First parachute release button*

*Second parachute release button*

*Stopwatch*

*Foot-rest*

*Engine starter button*

*Filtered air breathing bottle*

## ...the controls

...ble breathed filtered air through a mask ...he drove. In front of him there was a ...ke-shaped steering wheel, an accelerator ...d brake pedal, parachute release controls, ...d various gauges. The designers had ...n very optimistic – his speedometer ...ld read up to 800 mph (1,287.4 km/h)!

*Air mask*

*Yoke-shaped steering wheel*

*Accelerator pedal*

15

# MALLARD

IMAGINE YOU'RE SITTING BY A STRETCH OF ENGLANI
London and North Eastern Railway on a summer day. It is July 3, 1938. Suddenly a train headed
a sleek blue locomotive streaks by, moving faster than anything you have ever seen. The engine
number 4468, is named Mallard, and has just set the world speed record for steam locomotives,
126 mph (202 km/h). Designed by Sir Nigel Gresley,
Mallard was an A4 class locomotive designed to
pull express trains. Mallard is preserved today
in England's National Railway Museum.

### Sleek machine
For his A4s, Gresley designed a streamlined casin
Inspired by race cars, the casing reduced air
resistance and helped the locos reach high speed

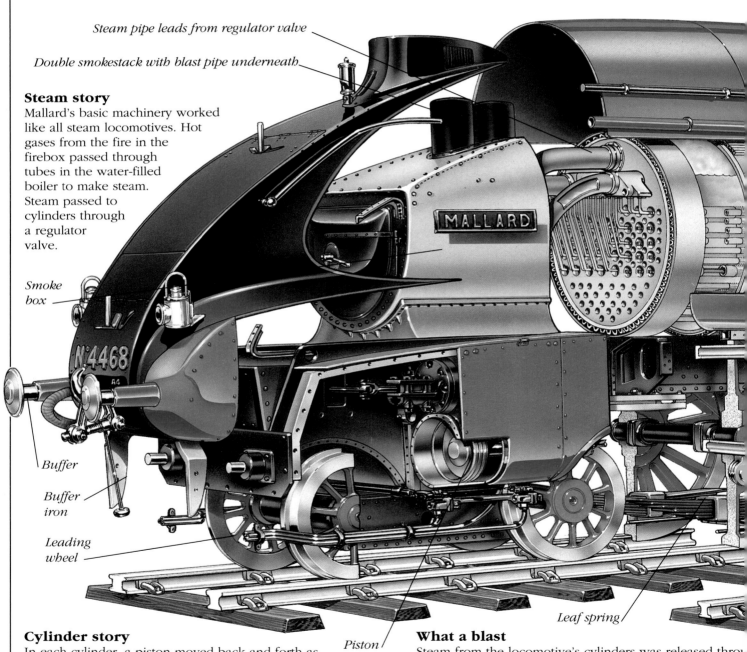

*Steam pipe leads from regulator valve*

*Double smokestack with blast pipe underneath*

### Steam story
Mallard's basic machinery worked
like all steam locomotives. Hot
gases from the fire in the
firebox passed through
tubes in the water-filled
boiler to make steam.
Steam passed to
cylinders through
a regulator
valve.

*Smoke
box*

*Buffer*

*Buffer
iron*

*Leading
wheel*

*Leaf spring*

*Piston
inside left-
hand
cylinder*

### Cylinder story
In each cylinder, a piston moved back and forth as
steam was let in at one side or the other by a system
of valves. The back-and-forth action of each piston
drove the wheels through the driving rods.

### What a blast
Steam from the locomotive's cylinders was released throu
the blast pipe, creating a partial vacuum that drew hot ga
along the boiler tubes and up the smokestack. This also
drew air into the firebox and made the fire burn hotter.

# TECHNICAL DATA

WIDTH OVER FOOTPLATE:
9 FT (2.7 M)

WEIGHT:
147,840 LB (67,060 KG)

MAXIMUM SPEED:
126 MPH (202 KM/H)

HEIGHT:
3 FT 1 IN (3.98 M)

LENGTH WITH TENDER:
71 FT (21.6 M)

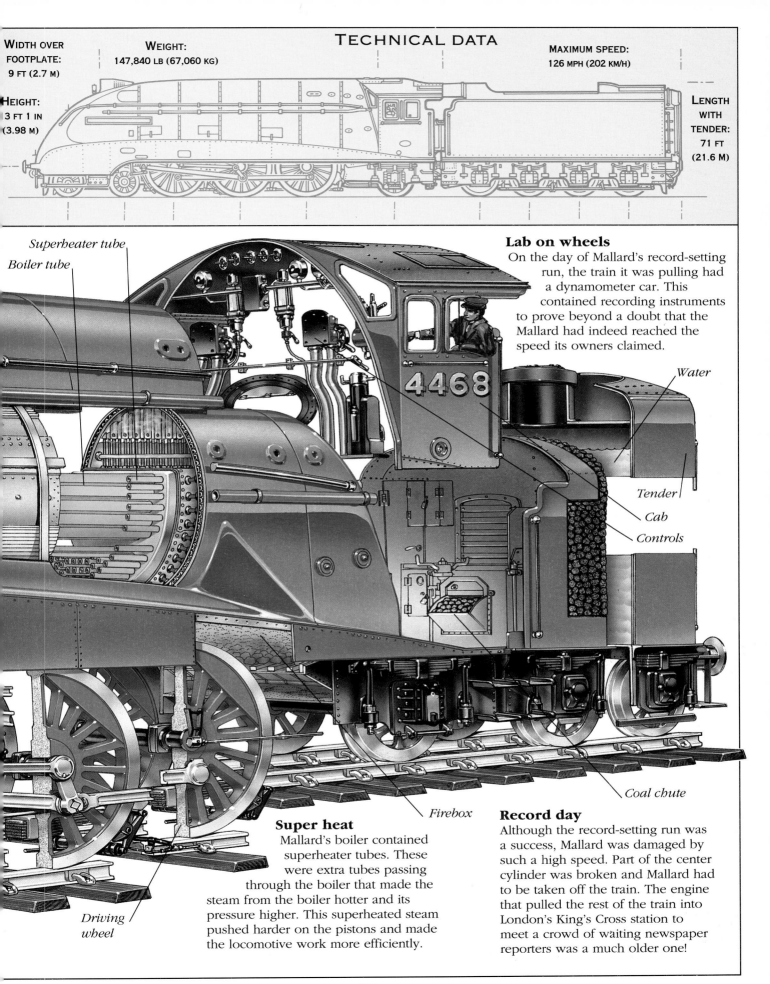

*Superheater tube*

*Boiler tube*

4468

*Driving wheel*

*Firebox*

*Water*

*Tender*

*Cab*

*Controls*

*Coal chute*

## Lab on wheels
On the day of Mallard's record-setting run, the train it was pulling had a dynamometer car. This contained recording instruments to prove beyond a doubt that the Mallard had indeed reached the speed its owners claimed.

## Super heat
Mallard's boiler contained superheater tubes. These were extra tubes passing through the boiler that made the steam from the boiler hotter and its pressure higher. This superheated steam pushed harder on the pistons and made the locomotive work more efficiently.

## Record day
Although the record-setting run was a success, Mallard was damaged by such a high speed. Part of the center cylinder was broken and Mallard had to be taken off the train. The engine that pulled the rest of the train into London's King's Cross station to meet a crowd of waiting newspaper reporters was a much older one!

# TURBINIA

IN JUNE 1897 THE WORLD'S BIGGEST NAVY WAS putting on a show at Spithead, England, to celebrate Queen Victoria's Diamond Jubilee. Lines of warships, the pride of the British Royal Navy, were smartly lined up for a review watched by representatives from around the world. Suddenly a small private boat appeared and sped up and down the lines. The onlookers were amazed as they watched the fastest boat in the world. The boat was the *Turbinia*, built by Charles Parsons to show his new invention, the steam turbine marine engine. His brilliant sales demonstration that day changed the world of shipping forever.

## The new design

In Parsons's engine a coal-fired boiler heated water to make steam. The steam was forced through blades fitted around a shaft with a propeller on the end. The blades spun around, turning the shaft and the propeller. The new turbine engine was lighter, more efficient, and quieter than older types of steam engines.

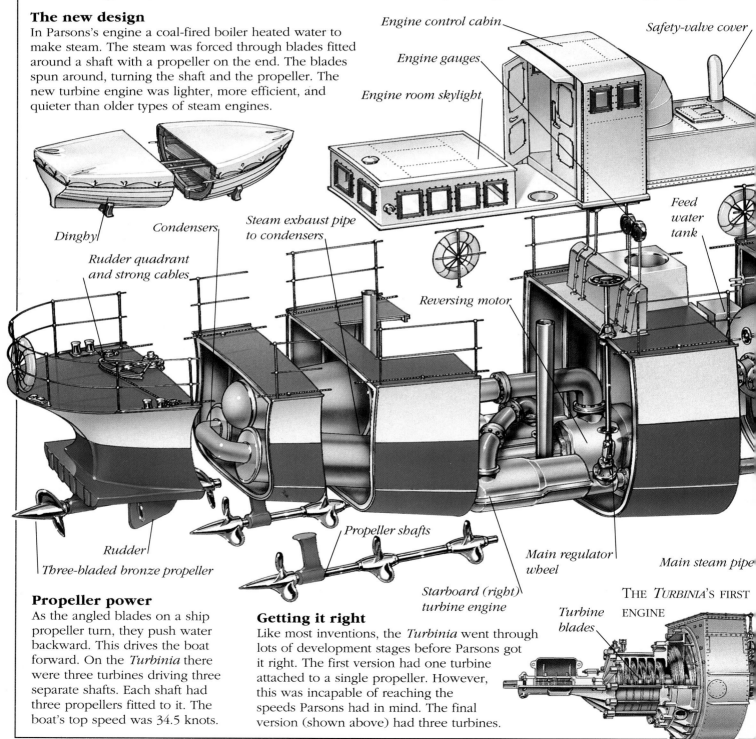

Engine control cabin

Engine gauges

Engine room skylight

Safety-valve cover

Feed water tank

Dinghy

Condensers

Steam exhaust pipe to condensers

Reversing motor

Rudder quadrant and strong cables

Rudder

Three-bladed bronze propeller

Propeller shafts

Main regulator wheel

Main steam pipe

Starboard (right) turbine engine

Turbine blades

THE *TURBINIA*'S FIRST ENGINE

## Propeller power

As the angled blades on a ship propeller turn, they push water backward. This drives the boat forward. On the *Turbinia* there were three turbines driving three separate shafts. Each shaft had three propellers fitted to it. The boat's top speed was 34.5 knots.

## Getting it right

Like most inventions, the *Turbinia* went through lots of development stages before Parsons got it right. The first version had one turbine attached to a single propeller. However, this was incapable of reaching the speeds Parsons had in mind. The final version (shown above) had three turbines.

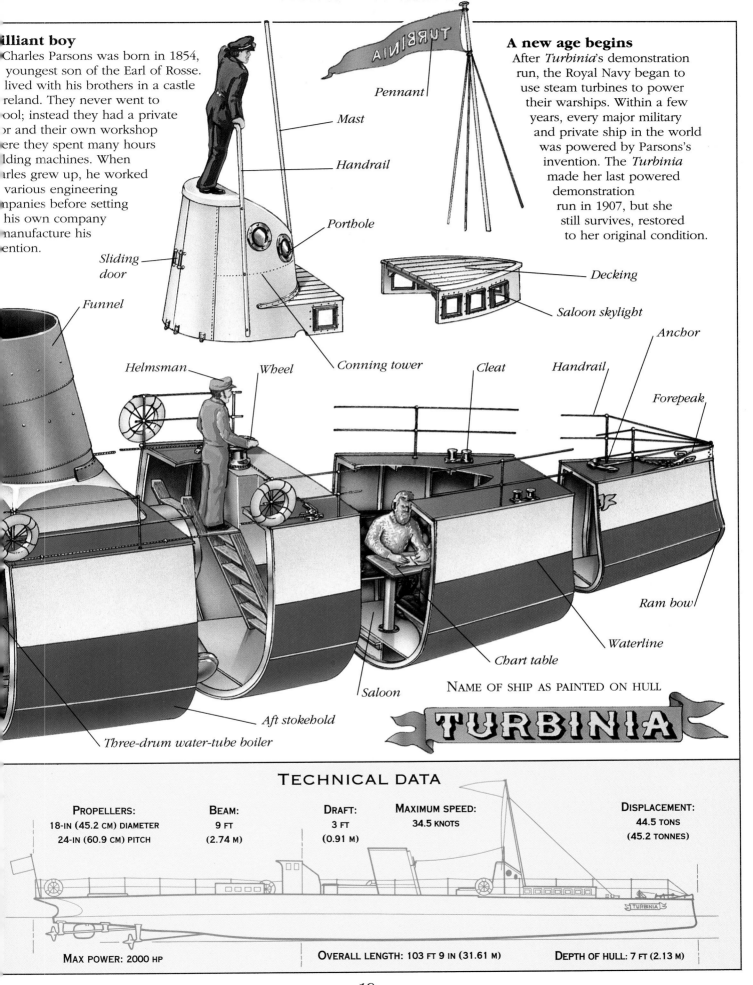

## illiant boy

Charles Parsons was born in 1854,
youngest son of the Earl of Rosse.
lived with his brothers in a castle
reland. They never went to
ool; instead they had a private
or and their own workshop
ere they spent many hours
lding machines. When
rles grew up, he worked
various engineering
npanies before setting
his own company
manufacture his
ention.

## A new age begins

After *Turbinia*'s demonstration
run, the Royal Navy began to
use steam turbines to power
their warships. Within a few
years, every major military
and private ship in the world
was powered by Parsons's
invention. The *Turbinia*
made her last powered
demonstration
run in 1907, but she
still survives, restored
to her original condition.

Pennant

Mast

Handrail

Porthole

Sliding door

Funnel

Conning tower

Decking

Saloon skylight

Anchor

Handrail

Forepeak

Helmsman

Wheel

Cleat

Ram bow

Waterline

Chart table

Saloon

Aft stokehold

Three-drum water-tube boiler

NAME OF SHIP AS PAINTED ON HULL

**TURBINIA**

## TECHNICAL DATA

**PROPELLERS:**
18-IN (45.2 CM) DIAMETER
24-IN (60.9 CM) PITCH

**BEAM:**
9 FT
(2.74 M)

**DRAFT:**
3 FT
(0.91 M)

**MAXIMUM SPEED:**
34.5 KNOTS

**DISPLACEMENT:**
44.5 TONS
(45.2 TONNES)

**MAX POWER:** 2000 HP

**OVERALL LENGTH:** 103 FT 9 IN (31.61 M)

**DEPTH OF HULL:** 7 FT (2.13 M)

# DRAG BIKE

FOR SHEER EXCITEMENT AND DANGER, MOTORCYCLE DRAG RACING is one of the ultimate experiences! With very little protection, riders sit astride super-charged monster machines knowing that one small error could prove disastrous. Once drag bikes raced against drag cars, but now drag bikes race in pairs over a 1,320-ft (402-m) straight course at speeds of nearly 200 mph (325 km/h). The riders need practice, planning, skill, and, above all, courage to explore the limits of their bikes' performance.

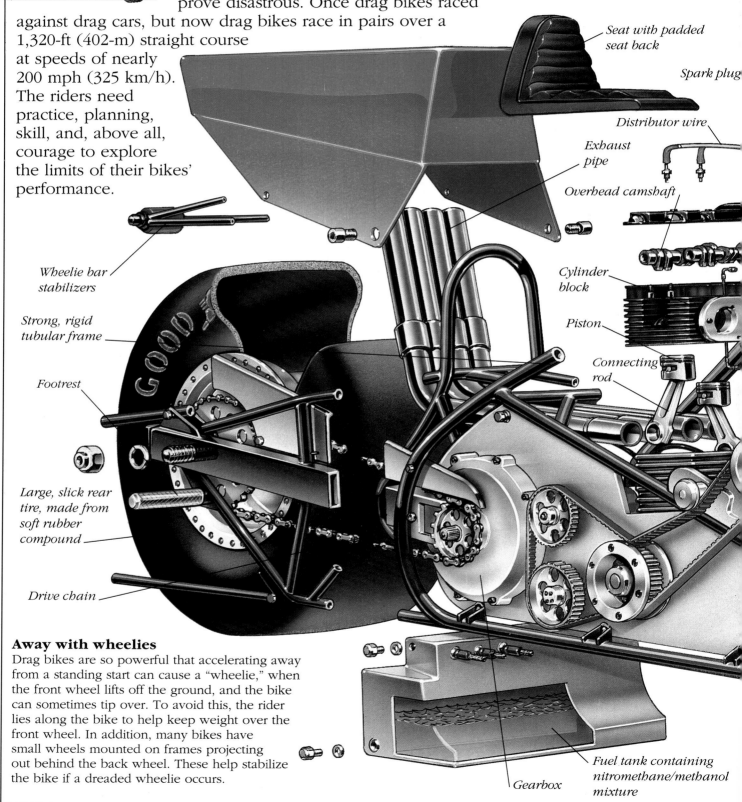

Seat with padded seat back

Spark plug

Distributor wire

Exhaust pipe

Overhead camshaft

Cylinder block

Piston

Connecting rod

Wheelie bar stabilizers

Strong, rigid tubular frame

Footrest

Large, slick rear tire, made from soft rubber compound

Drive chain

Gearbox

Fuel tank containing nitromethane/methanol mixture

## Away with wheelies

Drag bikes are so powerful that accelerating away from a standing start can cause a "wheelie," when the front wheel lifts off the ground, and the bike can sometimes tip over. To avoid this, the rider lies along the bike to help keep weight over the front wheel. In addition, many bikes have small wheels mounted on frames projecting out behind the back wheel. These help stabilize the bike if a dreaded wheelie occurs.

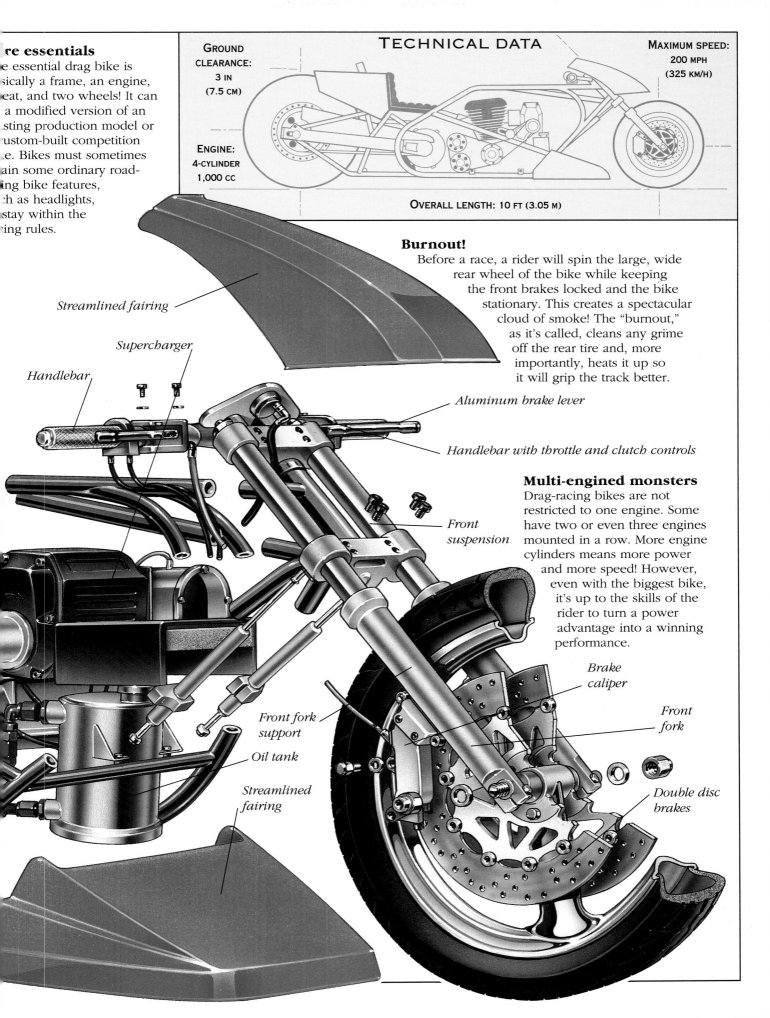

**re essentials**

e essential drag bike is
sically a frame, an engine,
eat, and two wheels! It can
a modified version of an
sting production model or
ustom-built competition
e. Bikes must sometimes
ain some ordinary road-
ng bike features,
ch as headlights,
stay within the
ing rules.

## TECHNICAL DATA

GROUND
CLEARANCE:
3 IN
(7.5 CM)

ENGINE:
4-CYLINDER
1,000 CC

MAXIMUM SPEED:
200 MPH
(325 KM/H)

OVERALL LENGTH: 10 FT (3.05 M)

*Streamlined fairing*

*Supercharger*

*Handlebar*

## Burnout!

Before a race, a rider will spin the large, wide
rear wheel of the bike while keeping
the front brakes locked and the bike
stationary. This creates a spectacular
cloud of smoke! The "burnout,"
as it's called, cleans any grime
off the rear tire and, more
importantly, heats it up so
it will grip the track better.

*Aluminum brake lever*

*Handlebar with throttle and clutch controls*

## Multi-engined monsters

Drag-racing bikes are not
restricted to one engine. Some
have two or even three engines
mounted in a row. More engine
cylinders means more power
and more speed! However,
even with the biggest bike,
it's up to the skills of the
rider to turn a power
advantage into a winning
performance.

*Front
suspension*

*Brake
caliper*

*Front
fork*

*Front fork
support*

*Oil tank*

*Streamlined
fairing*

*Double disc
brakes*

# POWERBOAT

### OFFSHORE POWERBOATS ARE THE SLEEK

monsters of water sports. They race over the open sea on courses that can be up to 160 miles (257 km) long. Some are monohulled (with one hull) and some, like the boat shown here, are catamarans, which means they have two narrow parallel hulls. They bounce over the ocean surface at speeds well over 100 mph (160 km/h). Powerboat racing is not for the timid. The boat frame and crew must be strong enough to endure fierce and constant battering during a race.

*Exhaust pipe*

*V-12 Lamborghini engine*

### Thirsty work

Racing powerboats use either inboard or outboard engines. An outboard engine is one attached and hinged onto the back of the boat. The craft shown here has two V-12 Lamborghini engines mounted inboard, which means they are positioned inside the boat's frame. These engines are very powerful, and also very thirsty. They can use 48 gal (181 l) of fuel per hour when racing!

*Transom takes the force of the pushing propellers*

*Engine exhaust outlets*

*Streamlined exhaust cowling*

*Hydraulic ram steers boat*

*Trim flap controls angle of boat in water*

*Fuel tank*

## TECHNICAL DATA

**PROPULSION:**
SURFACE DRIVE
WAVE-PIERCING PROPELLER

**CONSTRUCTION:**
ALUMINUM SHEET ON WELDED ALUMINUM FRAME

**ENGINES:**
2 X V-12 LAMBORGHINI 8.2-LITER
950 HP EACH

**LENGTH:**
50 FT (15.2 M)

## In the cockpit

Boats of this size usually need two crew members to control them. In this catamaran the driver sits in front with the throttle operator behind. The cockpit is surrounded by a clear canopy that helps streamline the boat and gives the crew a wide field of vision. It's based on a US F-16 jet fighter canopy, with the modification of an escape hole in the top in case of emergency.

VIEW OF COCKPIT

## The kill switch

As part of race regulations, each crew member must wear a "kill-switch" cord attached to one wrist. If they are thrown out of the boat, the kill-switch cord will automatically stop the engine so the boat does not veer across the ocean out of control.

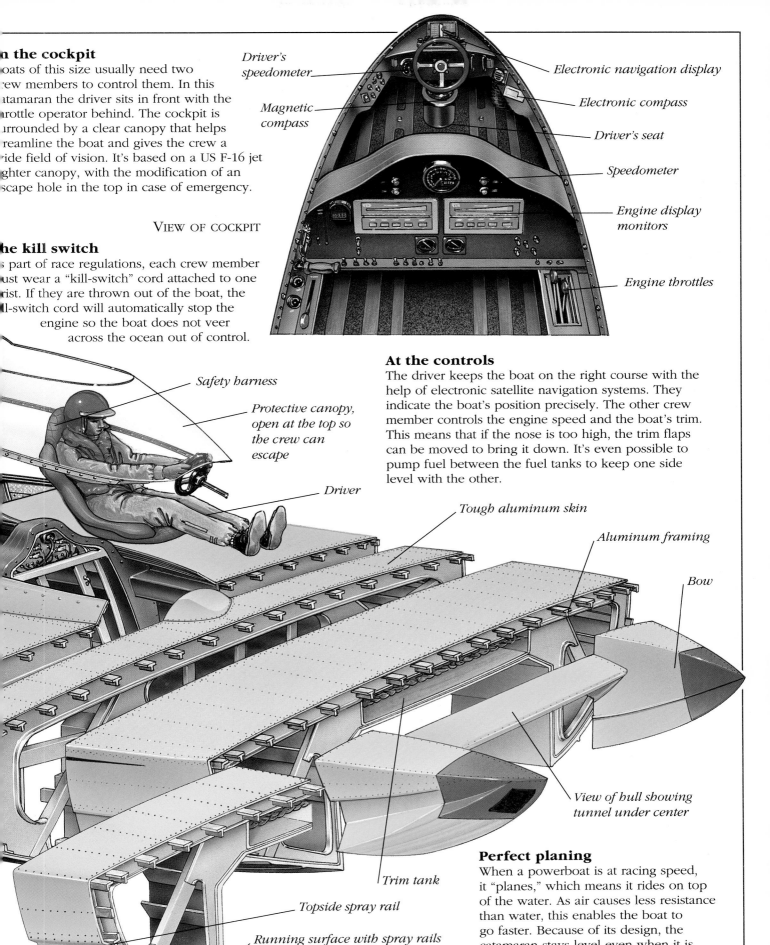

Driver's speedometer

Magnetic compass

Electronic navigation display

Electronic compass

Driver's seat

Speedometer

Engine display monitors

Engine throttles

Safety harness

Protective canopy, open at the top so the crew can escape

Driver

## At the controls

The driver keeps the boat on the right course with the help of electronic satellite navigation systems. They indicate the boat's position precisely. The other crew member controls the engine speed and the boat's trim. This means that if the nose is too high, the trim flaps can be moved to bring it down. It's even possible to pump fuel between the fuel tanks to keep one side level with the other.

Tough aluminum skin

Aluminum framing

Bow

View of hull showing tunnel under center

Trim tank

Topside spray rail

Running surface with spray rails

## Perfect planing

When a powerboat is at racing speed, it "planes," which means it rides on top of the water. As air causes less resistance than water, this enables the boat to go faster. Because of its design, the catamaran stays level even when it is turning, never breaking its air cushion.

# TEMPEST V

It is June 1944 and a pilot in England's Royal Air Force is straining his eyes to penetrate the darkness of the night sky. He is not looking for an enemy airplane, but an unmanned V-1 rocket, a deadly jet-powered "flying bomb." Suddenly the pilot sees a V-1's jet exhaust as a glimmer of light in the distance. The Hawker Tempest V aircraft he is flying is one of the only planes fast enough to catch it. Flying behind the bomb, he lines the exhaust up in his gunsight and fires, then turns quickly away as the V-1 explodes.

## High, fast, and deadly

V-1 flying bombs flew at an altitude between 1,500-2,000 ft (450-600 m). They were packed with explosives to wreak havoc when they fell to earth and blew up. The Hawker Tempests were the among the fastest propeller-powered planes of their day, fast enough to catch the bombs as they sped on their deadly journeys.

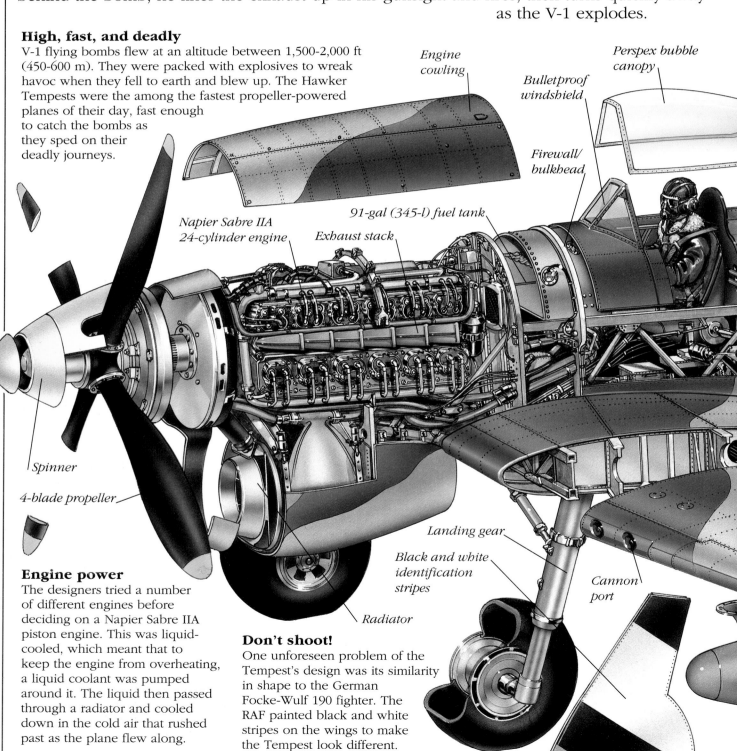

Engine cowling

Perspex bubble canopy

Bulletproof windshield

Firewall/ bulkhead

Napier Sabre IIA 24-cylinder engine

91-gal (345-l) fuel tank

Exhaust stack

Spinner

4-blade propeller

Landing gear

Black and white identification stripes

Cannon port

Radiator

## Engine power

The designers tried a number of different engines before deciding on a Napier Sabre IIA piston engine. This was liquid-cooled, which meant that to keep the engine from overheating, a liquid coolant was pumped around it. The liquid then passed through a radiator and cooled down in the cold air that rushed past as the plane flew along.

## Don't shoot!

One unforeseen problem of the Tempest's design was its similarity in shape to the German Focke-Wulf 190 fighter. The RAF painted black and white stripes on the wings to make the Tempest look different.

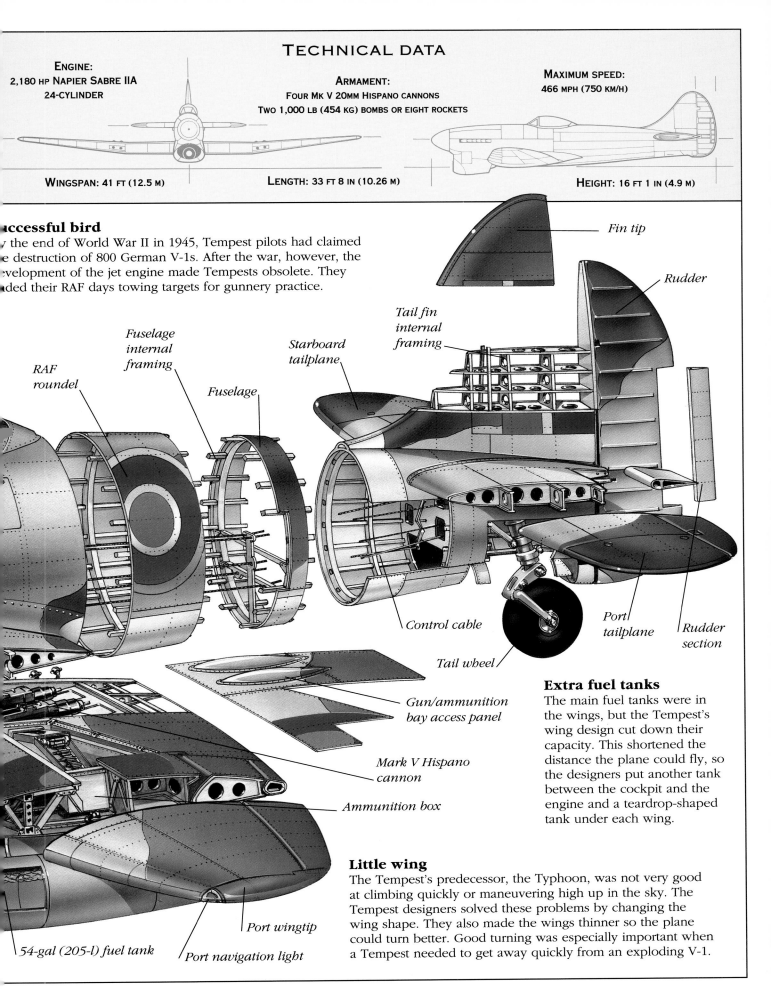

**ENGINE:**
2,180 HP NAPIER SABRE IIA
24-CYLINDER

**ARMAMENT:**
FOUR MK V 20MM HISPANO CANNONS
TWO 1,000 LB (454 KG) BOMBS OR EIGHT ROCKETS

**MAXIMUM SPEED:**
466 MPH (750 KM/H)

**WINGSPAN: 41 FT (12.5 M)**

**LENGTH: 33 FT 8 IN (10.26 M)**

**HEIGHT: 16 FT 1 IN (4.9 M)**

## uccessful bird

y the end of World War II in 1945, Tempest pilots had claimed
e destruction of 800 German V-1s. After the war, however, the
evelopment of the jet engine made Tempests obsolete. They
ded their RAF days towing targets for gunnery practice.

*Fin tip*

*Rudder*

*Tail fin internal framing*

*Starboard tailplane*

*Fuselage internal framing*

*Fuselage*

*RAF roundel*

*Control cable*

*Tail wheel*

*Gun/ammunition bay access panel*

*Mark V Hispano cannon*

*Ammunition box*

*Port tailplane*

*Rudder section*

*Port wingtip*

*Port navigation light*

*54-gal (205-l) fuel tank*

### Extra fuel tanks

The main fuel tanks were in
the wings, but the Tempest's
wing design cut down their
capacity. This shortened the
distance the plane could fly, so
the designers put another tank
between the cockpit and the
engine and a teardrop-shaped
tank under each wing.

### Little wing

The Tempest's predecessor, the Typhoon, was not very good
at climbing quickly or maneuvering high up in the sky. The
Tempest designers solved these problems by changing the
wing shape. They also made the wings thinner so the plane
could turn better. Good turning was especially important when
a Tempest needed to get away quickly from an exploding V-1.

# INDY CAR

INDY CAR RACING BEGAN IN THE UNITED STATES EARLY in the 1900s. It takes its name from the city of Indianapolis, Indiana, where a new speedway track was first used for racing in 1909. Today, Indy car racing is one of the most popular motor sports. The Indy car is heavier than the other well-known racing car, the Formula 1, and has a turbocharged engine that increases power output. Add to this aerodynamic features that hold the car to the track, and you have an amazing machine well able to withstand the speeds of 200 mph (322 km/h) regularly reached in an Indy car race.

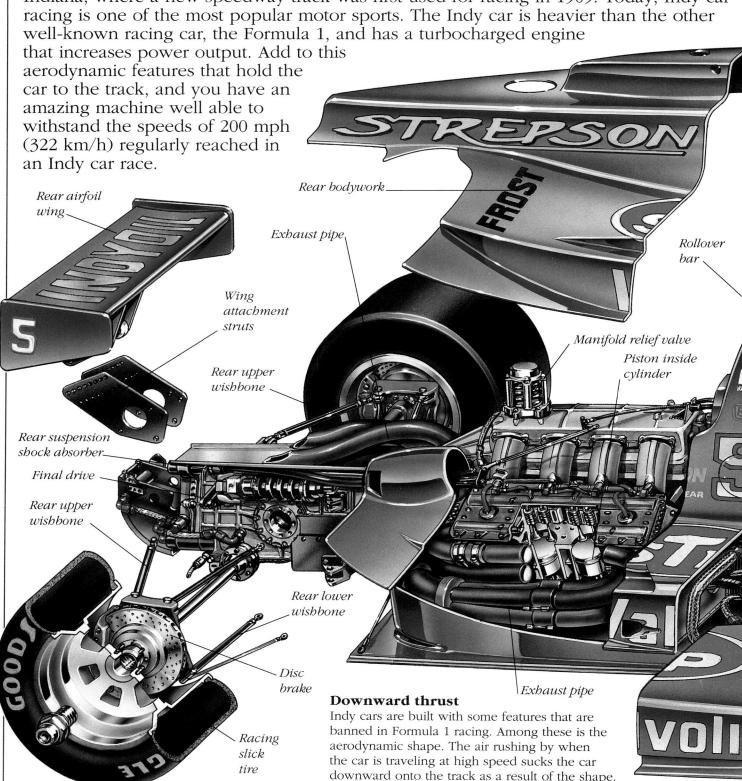

*Rear airfoil wing*

*Rear bodywork*

*Exhaust pipe*

*Rollover bar*

*Wing attachment struts*

*Rear upper wishbone*

*Manifold relief valve*

*Piston inside cylinder*

*Rear suspension shock absorber*

*Final drive*

*Rear upper wishbone*

*Rear lower wishbone*

*Disc brake*

*Exhaust pipe*

*Racing slick tire*

### Downward thrust
Indy cars are built with some features that are banned in Formula 1 racing. Among these is the aerodynamic shape. The air rushing by when the car is traveling at high speed sucks the car downward onto the track as a result of the shape.

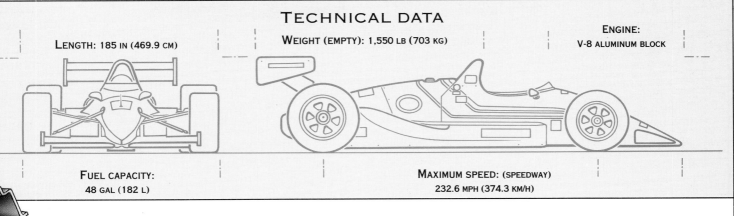

## TECHNICAL DATA

**LENGTH:** 185 IN (469.9 CM)

**WEIGHT (EMPTY):** 1,550 LB (703 KG)

**ENGINE:** V-8 ALUMINUM BLOCK

**FUEL CAPACITY:** 48 GAL (182 L)

**MAXIMUM SPEED: (SPEEDWAY)** 232.6 MPH (374.3 KM/H)

### Survival
The Indy car cockpit is made of carbon fiber to withstand impact and provide maximum protection for the driver in the event of a crash. The rollover bar provides protection for the driver's head.

### Instant elevation
Indy cars are specially built to cope with the banking (elevation on the outside) of the oval track. At the flick of a switch an Indy car driver can elevate the right side of the car using compressed air to compensate for the elevation.

### High-tech
The driver has a liquid-crystal display attached to the steering wheel. This gives details of engine rpm, engine and oil temperature, oil pressure, and other functions.

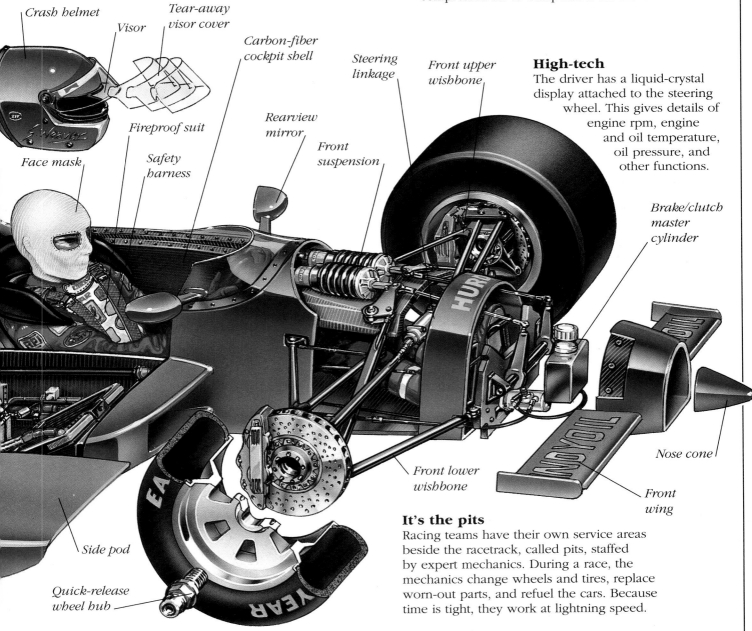

*Crash helmet*

*Visor*

*Tear-away visor cover*

*Carbon-fiber cockpit shell*

*Steering linkage*

*Front upper wishbone*

*Rearview mirror*

*Fireproof suit*

*Front suspension*

*Face mask*

*Safety harness*

*Brake/clutch master cylinder*

*Front lower wishbone*

*Nose cone*

*Front wing*

*Side pod*

*Quick-release wheel hub*

### It's the pits
Racing teams have their own service areas beside the racetrack, called pits, staffed by expert mechanics. During a race, the mechanics change wheels and tires, replace worn-out parts, and refuel the cars. Because time is tight, they work at lightning speed.

# SPEEDLINE

DURING THE LAST 150 YEARS, humans have reached ever-higher speeds in cars, trains, boats, and aircraft. People were afraid to travel in the first cars because of their speed, yet now many people fly in airliners going faster than the speed of sound. Here are some speed machine milestones.

*1885 BENZ TRICYCLE 8-10 MPH (12-16 KM/H)*

*1860 TEA CLIPPER 12 MPH (20 KM/H)*

*1990s INDY CAR 230 MPH (370 KM/H)*

*Supercharger*

*1990s DRAGSTER 230 MPH (370 KM/H)*

*1938 LNER MALLARD 125 MPH (201 KM/H)*

*Streamlined shape*

L N E R 4468

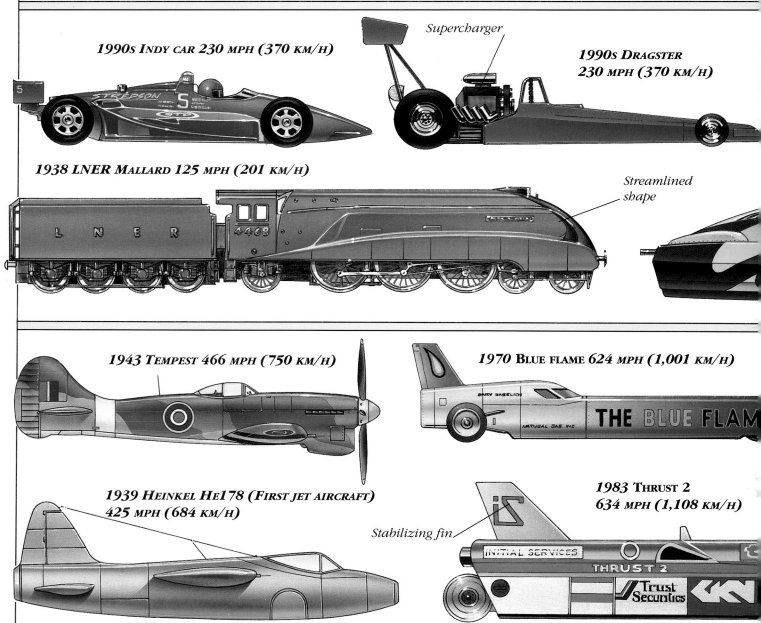

*1943 TEMPEST 466 MPH (750 KM/H)*

*1970 BLUE FLAME 624 MPH (1,001 KM/H)*

GARY GABELICH

NATURAL GAS INC.

THE BLUE FLAME

*1939 HEINKEL HE178 (FIRST JET AIRCRAFT) 425 MPH (684 KM/H)*

*1983 THRUST 2 634 MPH (1,108 KM/H)*

*Stabilizing fin*

INITIAL SERVICES

THRUST 2

Trust Securities

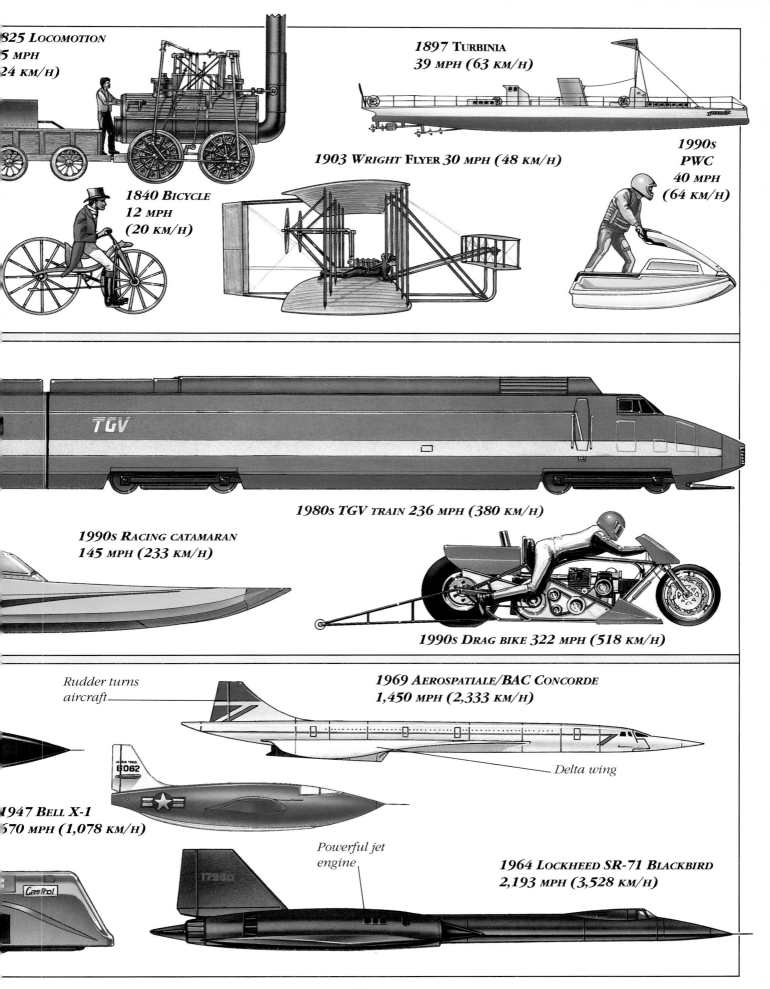

**825 LOCOMOTION**
5 MPH
24 KM/H)

**1897 TURBINIA**
39 MPH (63 KM/H)

**1840 BICYCLE**
12 MPH
(20 KM/H)

**1903 WRIGHT FLYER 30 MPH (48 KM/H)**

**1990s PWC**
40 MPH
(64 KM/H)

**1980s TGV TRAIN 236 MPH (380 KM/H)**

**1990s RACING CATAMARAN**
145 MPH (233 KM/H)

**1990s DRAG BIKE 322 MPH (518 KM/H)**

Rudder turns aircraft

**1969 AEROSPATIALE/BAC CONCORDE**
1,450 MPH (2,333 KM/H)

Delta wing

**1947 BELL X-1**
570 MPH (1,078 KM/H)

Powerful jet engine

**1964 LOCKHEED SR-71 BLACKBIRD**
2,193 MPH (3,528 KM/H)

# GLOSSARY

### Acceleration
The rate at which a vehicle or a craft picks up speed.

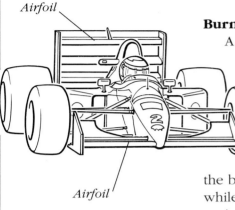

*Airfoil*

*Airfoil*

### Airfoil
A winglike structure on a car or plane. As a vehicle travels along, an airfoil forces air more quickly over one side than the other, depending on its shape. This creates either lift (as with a plane) or a downward force (as with a race car).

### Air-resistance
The pushing force exerted by air as an object moves through it. Speed machine designers try to keep this low so that it won't slow a moving vehicle down.

### Ballast
Heavy material such as stone and iron used to steady a ship and make sure it sits evenly in the water, without leaning to one side or the other.

### Boiler
The part of a steam engine in which the water is heated up to make steam.

### Burnout
A technique used in drag racing to warm up the large rear tires. Using water to lubricate them, the back tires are spun while the vehicle is stationary. This cleans the tires and heats the tire rubber so it will grip the track better.

### Catamaran
A boat with two parallel narrow hulls, one on either side. This cuts down on water resistance and helps the boat go faster.

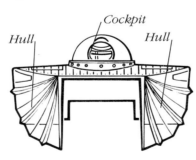

*Cockpit*

*Hull* *Hull*

CATAMARAN

### Cylinder
Part of an engine. It is a tubular chamber in which a piston is pushed in and out by the force of steam or hot gas entering the cylinder under pressure.

### Disc brake
In this type of braking system, brake pads clamp on to a disk attached to a vehicle wheel. The resulting friction slows the wheel down.

### Elapsed time
The time taken by a drag car or a drag bike to complete a run of a quarter of a mile.

### Exhaust
The waste gases expelled from the cylinders of an engine once fuel has been burned in them.

### Fuel tank
A chamber where fuel is kept. When a vehicle is started, fuel travels from the tank via pipes to the engine.

### G-force
The action of gravity on the human body, normally measured as 1. The effect of maneuvering in a high-speed craft can increase this measurement. For instance, a g-force of 8 (as experienced in a racing powerboat) means that the body weighs effectively eight times its normal weight.

### Inboard
The term used when a powerboat engine is positioned inside a boat's frame.

### Internal combustion engine
A type of engine that works by burning (combusting) fuel within metal cylinders inside the engine. Inside each cylinder, a metal barrel called a piston is moved up or down by the forces caused by the burning fuel. The motion of the piston powers other parts of the vehicle.

INTERNAL COMBUSTION ENGINE

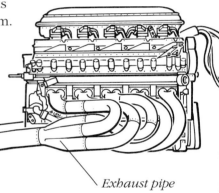

*Exhaust pipe*

### Jet engine
An engine that produces a powerful jet of hot gas (as in a plane) or water (as in a PWC) to push a vehicle or craft along.

### Nitromethane
A particularly rich fuel used in drag racing engines. It burns very efficiently, helping increase the engine's power output.

### Outboard
The term used when a powerboat engine is positioned outside a boat at the back.

**...ston**
...metal barrel inside
...cylinder. It is pushed
... or down in the cylinder
... forces caused by
...rning fuel (as in a
...mbustion engine) or
... oil pumped into the
...inder (as in a
...draulic system).

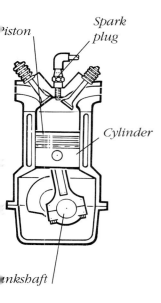

*Piston*

*Spark plug*

*Cylinder*

*...nkshaft*

CUTAWAY OF ENGINE

**...rsonal watercraft**
...VC for short. A kind of
...otorcycle on water skis,
...ed in water sports. One
...rticular make of PWC
...called a Jet Ski.

...WC

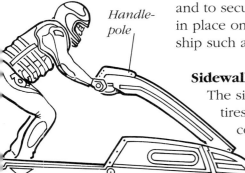

*Handle-pole*

**Planing**
The combined effect of
speed and construction
that allows boats to
skim across the water's
surface by raising
them up on a very
thin cushion of air. Air
provides less resistance
than water, so a boat
can travel faster if
it planes.

**Propeller**
A set of blades mounted
on a spinning shaft. The
spinning action creates
forces that push a craft
through air or water.

**Radiator**
Part of an engine cooling
system. Heat generated
by a working engine is
drawn off by a coolant
liquid that circulates
around the engine.
Heat passes out into
the air as the
coolant travels through
the radiator. Then the
cooled-down coolant flows
back around the engine
to do its job again.

**Running rigging**
A system of ropes used
to lift the yards and sails
and to secure the sails
in place on a sailing
ship such as a clipper.

**Sidewalls**
The side surfaces of
tires. They do not
come into contact
with track
or road
surface.

**Standing rigging**
A system of ropes or wire
cables used to hold the
masts of a sailing ship
firmly in place.

**Streamlining**
The smooth design of
a speed machine, which
enables it to move more
quickly by keeping air
or water resistance to a
minimum as it travels
along. Air or water
resistance gets higher
if there are more
flat surfaces to push
against. It gets lower
if there is a smooth
surface to travel around.

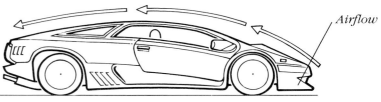

*Airflow*

STREAMLINING

**Supercharger**
This is sometimes
called a blower. It is a
device to help an engine
produce more power by
forcing a fuel vapor and
air mixture into the
engine under greatly
increased pressure.

**Supersonic**
Faster than the speed
of sound. Jet planes are
now supersonic and
record-breaking

supersonic land speed
vehicles are
being designed.

**Terminal velocity**
The highest speed reached
by a drag car or a drag
bike during a run over
a quarter-mile course.

**Throttle**
The device that controls
the flow of fuel into an
engine, causing it to
either speed up or
slow down.

**Trim**
The angle at which a
boat sits in the water.

**Wheelie**
As a result of
accelerating very
quickly on a motorcycle,
the front wheel comes up
off the ground and the
bike performs a wheelie.
The acceleration of drag
bikes is so quick that
many have "wheelie bars"
behind the rear wheel to
stop them from flipping
over.

WHEELIE

# INDEX

## A

A4 locomotive, 16
acceleration, 10, 11
aerodynamic shape, 26
airfoils
    dragster, 11
    Indy car, 27
airplane
    Blackbird, 6-7
    Tempest V, 24-25
altitude record, 7

## B

ballast, 9
banking, 27
boat
    powerboat, 22-23
    *Turbinia*, 18-19
boiler
    Mallard, 16, 17
    *Turbinia*, 18
Blackbird, 6-7
blower, 10
blower bags, 10
braking systems
    dragster, 11
    *Thrust 2*, 15
burnout
    dragster, 10

## C

car
    dragster, 10-11
    Indy car, 26-27
    *Thrust 2*, 14-15
catamaran, 22
clipper, 8-9
cockpit
    Indy car, 27
    powerboat, 23
crew
    Blackbird, 6
    powerboat, 23

## D

drag bike, 20-21
drag racing, 10, 20
dragster, 10-11

## E

elevation, 27
engine
    cylinder, 24
    impeller, 12
    inboard/outboard, 22
    jet, 14
    on Blackbird, 7
    steam turbine marine, 18
    supercharged, 10, 21
    turbocharged, 26

## F G

flying bombs, 24
flying suits, 6
friction, 6
fuel
    in inboard/outboard engines, 22
    JP7, 7
    nitromethane/methanol, 11
fuel tanks
    powerboat, 23
    Tempest V, 25

Gresley, Sir Nigel, 16

## H

Hawker Tempest, 24

## I

ignition, chemical, 7
impeller, 12
Indianapolis, USA, 26
Indy car, 26-27
iron, 8

## J

J58 engine, 7
Jacobson, Clay, 12
Johnson, Lyndon, 6

## KL

Kawasaki Jet Ski, 12
kill switch, 23

locomotive, 16-17

## M

mach 3.2, 6
Mallard, 16-17
masters, 9
monohulled, 22

## N

Napier Sabre IIA engine, 24
naval review, 18
Noble, Richard, 14

## P

parachutes
    dragster, 11
    *Thrust 2*, 15
Parsons, Charles, 18, 19
personal watercraft (PWC), 12-13
pits, 27
planing, 23
powerboat, 22-23
Pratt and Whitney J58 engine, 7
propellers, 18

## R

races
    drag bike 20
    dragster, 10
    Indy car, 26
    powerboat, 22
    tea clipper, 9
racing teams, 27
radar, 6
reconnaissance plane, 6
roll-over bar, 27
Rolls-Royce Avon 302 jet engine, 14
run-out strip, 11

## S

sailing ship, 8-9
speed of sound, 6
speeds
    acceleration, 10, 11
    air, 6, 7
    cruising, 12
    land, 14, 16, 20, 26
    water, 18, 22
SR-71; *see* Blackbird
stabilizers, 20
steam locomotive, 16-17
supercharger, 10

## T

tea clipper, 8-9
Tempest V, 24-25
*Thrust 2*, 14-15
tires
    drag bike, 21
    dragster, 10
Top Fuel dragster, 10-11
trim, 31
    powerboat, 23
    tea clipper, 9
*Turbinia*, 18-19

## V

V-1 rocket, 24, 25
V-12 Lamborghini engine,

## W

wheelie, 20, 31

## Acknowledgments

Dorling Kindersley would like to thank the following people who helped in the preparation of this book:

Gary Biggin for additional line artwork
Lynn Bresler for the index
Cougar Marine
Kawasaki Motors (UK) Limited
Museum of British Road Transport, Coventry
Tyne and Wear Museums